JEFF BEZOS

THE FOUNDER OF amazon.com

JEFF BEZOS

THE FOUNDER OF amazon.com

ANN BYERS

The Rosen Publishing Group, Inc., New York

To my son Andy, who is one of Amazon.com's most loyal customers

Published in 2007 by The Rosen Publishing Group, Inc.
29 East 21st Street, New York, NY 10010

First Edition

Library of Congress Cataloging-in-Publication Data

Byers, Ann.
Jeff Bezos: the founder of Amazon.com/Ann Byers.—1st ed.
    p. cm.—(Internet career biographies)
Includes bibliographical references and index.
ISBN 1-4042-0717-1 (lib. bdg.)
1. Bezos, Jeffrey—Juvenile literature. 2. Amazon.com (Firm)—History—Juvenile literature. 3. Booksellers and bookselling—United States—Biography—Juvenile literature. 4. Businessmen—United States—Biography—Juvenile literature. 5. Internet bookstores—United States—History—Juvenile literature. 6. Electronic commerce—United States—History—Juvenile literature. I. Title. II. Series.
Z473.B47B94 2006
381'.4500202854678—dc22

                                                2005029236

Manufactured in the United States of America

On the cover: Jeff Bezos holds a copy of Douglas Hofstadter's *Fluid Concepts and Creative Analogies: Computer Models of the Fundamental Mechanisms of Thought*, the first title ever sold by Amazon.com.

Contents

The date: December 1997. The place: Amelia Island, a thirteen-mile strip of beaches, trees, and golf courses just off the northeastern edge of Florida. The destination: The Flash Foods Convenience Store. The mission: Who knew?

The car that pulled into the parking lot looked like dozens of others on this resort island. It was a white Chevrolet Suburban, large enough to hold four adults, and fast enough for a quick getaway. The people in the car did not appear unusual. Anyone would have thought this was a typical tourist family stopping by the convenience store for some forgotten item.

But when the Suburban pulled up to the convenience store, the female driver did not shut off the engine. The three men jumped quickly from the vehicle. One posted himself at the front door, obviously on the lookout. Another raced to the checkout line. The third shot to the back of the store. Their walkie-talkies crackled with hastily whispered code words. The woman at the wheel checked her watch, timing the raid. Within two minutes the three operatives were back in the car. They laughed heartily as they sped away with their purchase: a carton of milk.

Jeff Bezos pushes a shopping cart piled high with products available on the Amazon.com Web site. In his "store," people fill online "shopping carts" from online "shelves." This photo was taken in September 1998, three months after Amazon began to offer its customers music CDs and DVDs in addition to books.

Who were these four people having so much fun turning a milk run into a commando mission? The mother was the daughter of a high-level administrator of the Atomic Energy Commission. At the time of the milk raid, the father was an engineer for a major oil company. Their daughter was not with them on this excursion, but their two sons were. The youngest was a partner in a creative advertising agency in New York.

It was the oldest son, however, who took the family's taste for wild adventure to the extreme. He had quit a high-paying job in the financial industry and moved all the way across the country. He had spent a full year building a company that did something no one had heard of. And after only two years in business, he had already lost millions of dollars. But he had a positive outlook that kept him going. In fact, his optimistic attitude became the motto for his company: "Work hard, have fun, and make history."

The world would soon know him as one of the hardest working, most fun-loving men of the Internet age. He would make history in two years as *Time* magazine's Person of the Year. To his family, however, he was known in their spy games by his code name, Ffej Sozeb. It is his name spelled backward.

CHAPTER ONE

EARLY ADVENTURES

For Jeff's father, Mike Bezos, there was a time when military raids were not a game. He lived in Cuba, an island country just off the coast of Florida. For much of Mike's childhood, Cuba was wracked by warring political armies. When Fidel Castro seized power in 1959, many Cubans feared that his government would take their children from them or harm them. They wanted to send their children to the United States, where they would be safe.

A Catholic priest put together a plan. Called "Pedro Pan," the operation brought thousands of children ages six to seventeen to the United States. Mike was one of them. He was a teenager when he arrived in 1962. Like the others, he came without parents and he spoke no English. All he owned were the clothes he was wearing and one extra shirt. When he arrived, he was housed in a mission with fifteen other Cuban refugees.

Mike learned English and he finished high school. He then moved to Albuquerque, New Mexico, to study engineering. To earn a living while he was going to college, he took a job as a night clerk in a bank. There he worked with a pretty woman named Jackie Gise Jorgensen.

Father Bryan O. Walsh was the mastermind behind the Pedro Pan operation that brought Mike Bezos to the United States. Here, Walsh poses with a young Cuban boy in front of a mission home in Miami, Florida. The home housed some of the more than 14,000 children who came to the United States from Cuba between December 1960 and October 1962.

Jackie was only seventeen at that time, and she was married. Not long after Mike and Jackie met, on January 12, 1964, Jackie gave birth to a boy she named Jeff. Soon after her baby was born, however, her husband left the two of them.

Over the course of the next four years, Mike and Jackie fell in love and eventually married. After their wedding, Mike wanted to adopt her son. So, when he was four years old, Jeff legally became Jeffrey Preston Bezos.

Jeff does not know or have any memory of his birth father. "I've never been curious about him," he has said.[1] When he was ten, his mother and father explained to him that he was adopted, but that revelation did not bother Jeff. "My real father is the guy who raised me," he would tell people.[2] He has always been grateful to have Mike and Jackie as his parents.

THE LAZY G

Jeff's parents were not the only strong influences in his young life. Jeff also had a special bond with his mother's dad, Lawrence Preston Gise. He called his grandfather Pops. Pops had inherited a 25,000-acre (100 sq km) cattle ranch in Cotulla, Texas. When Jeff was four, his grandfather retired from his job and went to live on the ranch, which he called the Lazy G. Until he was sixteen, Jeff spent nearly every summer with his grandmother and Pops at the Lazy G.

The cattle ranch was a wonderful place for a city boy. It exposed Jeff to a world totally different from the concrete and bustle of the places he called home. Jeff's father had become an engineer with Exxon, a huge oil company. He received several job promotions that required the family to move often. Jeff was born in Albuquerque but spent much of his early childhood in Houston, Texas. The family then moved to Pensacola, Florida. During Jeff's high school years, the family moved once more, to Miami. But in the summer, Jeff would return to the quiet of the ranch. It felt to him like it was in the middle of nowhere. On the Lazy G, he could roam the open land and ride horses to his heart's content. In addition, he thought it was fun to drive Pops's International Harvester Scout long before he got his driver's license.

The ranch was not all play. Even as a small boy, Jeff learned to enjoy working hard. As soon as he was old enough to handle a branding iron, he stamped the "Lazy G" on Pops's cattle. He helped his grandfather vaccinate and take care of all the cows. He dug ditches and laid pipe. When something broke, he helped fix it. He learned how to repair pumps and windmills, sometimes without proper equipment or parts. Once, he and Pops read through a tall stack of mail-order repair manuals and figured out how to get a broken Caterpillar tractor running again. Another time, Pops bought a used bulldozer with a stripped transmission. In order to rebuild it, they had to remove a 500-pound gear. The only way to do it was to build their own crane, which they did.

Jeff's mother felt that summers on the ranch taught her son that "there really aren't any problems without solutions." It taught him that "obstacles are only obstacles if you think they're obstacles. Otherwise, they're opportunities."[3] Over the next several years, Jeff would encounter one obstacle after another. Each one he saw as a challenge, just waiting for a creative solution.

If Jeff was anything, he was creative. Sensing this, his grandfather nurtured Jeff's creative genius. He made the Lazy G more than a ranch; he made it a science lab as well. Before Jeff was born, Pops had worked for the U.S. Department of Defense and the Atomic Energy Commission. He had developed space technology and missile defense systems. So Jeff's grandfather knew how to build and operate very elaborate scientific machinery. With his background, Pops was able to keep his inquisitive grandson supplied with an endless array of educational games and science kits.

Young Inventor

Although Jeff learned much from the kits, he probably would have figured things out without them. He seemed to have been born with a thirst to analyze how things worked, to take them apart and put them back together in new ways. He was only three years old when his mother realized this about him. He had told her that he wanted to sleep in a bed, but she thought he was too young to move out of his crib. Undeterred, Jeff took matters into his own hands, and one day Jackie found the resourceful toddler with a screwdriver, attempting to take the bars off his crib.

The same analytical curiosity was evident in preschool. Jeff would be so involved in a task that he could not stop one activity when it was time for the next. His teachers had to physically pick him up, chair and all, and move him to the scheduled learning station.

To nurture his love of science and gadgets, Mike and Jackie enrolled their son in a special public school program for gifted children. It was twenty miles from their home in Houston, but the Bezoses thought the education was worth the drive.

One item at the school fascinated Jeff. It was a cube lined with mirrors. The mirrors had motors that made them move. Any object placed inside the cube was reflected multiple times from an endless number of constantly shifting angles. Looking into the cube was like being in space, like staring into infinity.

Jeff desperately wanted his own infinity cube. But $20 was more than his parents wanted to spend on what they thought was a toy or a passing fancy. Not seeing his parents' "no" as an obstacle, Jeff studied the school's cube and bought his own parts. He could afford mirrors and he could make motors. So Jeff built his own infinity cube.

It was only one of his many projects. Jeff went far beyond the amateur radio kits that he built early on. Once, he took an umbrella, stripped it of its fabric, and wrapped the skeleton in aluminum foil. When the sun heated the foil, the strange contraption became a solar cooker.

Another time he used an old vacuum cleaner to create a hovercraft, a vehicle that moved just above the surface of the ground. When his younger sister and brother were old enough to pester him, he rigged a buzzer to his bedroom door so he would know if they invaded his space. He turned the family's garage into his private laboratory and workshop. His mom and grandfather bought so many science kits and parts that Jackie once laughed, "I think single-handedly we kept many Radio Shacks in business."[4]

YOUNG ENTREPRENEUR

Invention was only one expression of Jeff's analytical personality. Another was his ability to look into the future, decide what he could do to make it better, and then do it. Jeff was by nature an entrepreneur—a person who has ideas for brand-new things and is willing to work to make those things happen. At his high school in Miami, Florida, he determined that he would be the student with the highest grades. So he studied, even though school was easy for him. He did extra projects and entered competitions, and in 1982, he graduated as valedictorian, tops in his class, just as he planned.

In high school, Jeff worked one summer at a McDonald's restaurant. But he was not content flipping hamburgers and cooking french fries. So the next summer, he started his first business. In partnership with Ursula Werner, his girlfriend at the time, he started a summer camp for fourth, fifth, and sixth graders. They called it the DREAM Institute. The letters stood for "Directed REAsoning Methods." It was to be an educational program that focused on science and literature. The two friends typed up an advertisement on an Apple II computer, offering the camp for two weeks, three hours a day, for a reasonable fee.

Five children signed up for the DREAM Institute, including Jeff's sister and brother. In Jeff's bedroom, they read *Gulliver's Travels*, *David Copperfield*, *The Lord of the Rings*, and other classic books and plays. They learned very practical skills, like how to operate a camera, and discussed complex issues such as space travel and limiting nuclear weapons. And Jeff learned first-hand that being an entrepreneur was far more rewarding than being a fry cook. From that time on, he would always have the dream of starting his own business.

Jeff Bezos, Student at Palmetto High School, Miami, Florida

- Won school's Best Science Student Award sophomore, junior, and senior years
- Won Best Math Student Award junior and senior years
- Won a trip to NASA's Marshall Space Flight Center in Huntsville, Alabama, with his essay "The Effect of Zero Gravity on the Aging Rate of the Common Housefly"
- With two other students, won the science prize in the Miami Herald Silver Knight competition for South Florida high school students, senior year
- Valedictorian of the class of 1982, graduating at the top of his class of 680 students

A Different Kind of Guy

Most of the things Jeff did, he did a little differently than everyone else. While his grade-school friends rode bikes or played arcade games, Jeff spent hours with an early *Star Trek* game on one of Houston's first computers. His high school buddies wanted to be policemen or pilots; he dreamed of becoming an astronaut or a physicist. Others thought of building houses or hotels; he seriously hoped he could build a space station someday.

Jeff's "different-ness" helped him over-come what would have been difficult hurdles to anyone less determined. A small boy who did not appear the least bit athletic, he barely met the weight requirement for his city's youth football league. Still, he signed up to play. To his parents' surprise, he became defensive captain of the team. He was made captain not because of his strength, but because he could remember what everyone was supposed to do on every play. Even in sports, in which he did not excel, Jeff stood out as exceptional.

In college, however, he did not stand out as much as he was used to. Jeff chose Princeton University for college because it had one of the best physics departments in the country. He had settled on becoming the next Einstein. He did well at Princeton. He was in an honors physics program and was a very strong student. But he was not number one. "It was really sort of a startling insight," he said, to realize that "there were three people in the class who were much, much better at it than I was."[5] Jeff wanted the challenge of being the best, so he changed his major to electrical engineering and computer science.

In that field, he was better than best. He graduated in 1986 summa cum laude, which

BLUE ORIGIN

Jeff Bezos never gave up his childhood dream of building a space station. In 2000, he founded Blue Origin, a company that, according to its Web site, is dedicated to "developing vehicles and technologies that, over time, will help enable an enduring human presence in space." His plan is to build a reusable spaceship that will carry people to the edge of space and back. He will build the spaceship on 165,000 acres of land he bought in west Texas. Bezos's high school business partner, Ursula Werner, believes the reason he founded Amazon.com was to make enough money to pursue this dream.

In 2004, Bezos bought the Longfellow cattle ranches in west Texas. The land is a good place for building and testing aircraft. Far from any city, it has both flat stretches and hills. Besides using the property for testing spaceships, Bezos hopes his children will enjoy summers on a Texas ranch, just as he did.

means "with highest honors." A perfect grade point average was 4.0, but in his department, Jeff scored 4.2. The extra points came from A-pluses.

At Princeton, as with everything else he did, Jeff Bezos lived by what would later become his three-part motto. He worked hard. He had fun. Now, with a degree in hand from a top-notch university, he was ready to make history.

CHAPTER TWO

WORKING HARD

J eff Bezos had no trouble finding a job. As a Princeton student with outstanding grades, he was offered employment with top firms before he even graduated. Intel, Bell Labs, and Andersen Consulting all wanted him to work for them. But Bezos was not interested in an ordinary, nine-to-five existence. He wanted adventure.

He thought he found it in an advertisement in Princeton's newspaper. A brand-new company on Wall Street was looking for the school's "best computer science graduates."[1] It was called Fitel because it combined finance and telecommunications. It worked with companies that were doing business between different countries. International business required complex communication because of the different languages and different currencies. The value of one country's money in another country could change by the minute. On large transactions, a small change in value could mean a big financial gain or loss. Super-fast and super-clear communication could make or save companies lots of money. Fitel was using computer programs to develop a communications network for buyers, sellers, banks, and investors that were doing business across national borders.

This was just the thing for Bezos. It was new and challenging. It demanded creativity. It was fast paced. He would start on the ground floor of something that could be big, that could make history. Immediately after graduating, in May 1986, he went to work for Fitel.

At first it was both hard and fun. Bezos traveled every week between New York and London. He opened an office in Tokyo. He designed, programmed, and tested. He made lots of money. But he did not see Fitel making history. And financial trading was not particularly exciting for him. So after two years he left for a position with another finance company, Bankers Trust.

BANKERS TRUST

Bankers Trust was a huge bank that managed money for large companies. By the time Bezos was twenty-six, he was the youngest vice president Bankers Trust had ever had. He developed a software program that was used by more than 100 of the biggest companies in the United States. It was a program that posted reports of the bank's activities so its customers could find out what was happening with their money before they received a written report in the mail. Although it was a rather crude program by today's standards, it was revolutionary then. Bezos was pleased with his accomplishment.

But not everyone at Bankers Trust was enthusiastic about the software. At that time—1988 and 1989—businesses stored their information on mainframe computers. These were gigantic pieces of hardware that took up entire rooms. Big companies did not trust their important data to a personal computer, or PC, that occupied only a

This tower is the headquarters of Bankers Trust Corporation, which hired Bezos in 1988. The forty-story building and its plaza take up an entire city block in downtown Manhattan. The huge structure projects to the world an image of importance and stability. Bezos abandoned that stability to start up Amazon.com, well before the Internet was a proven winner.

few feet on a desk. Such a small computer could not have enough power or memory to do the calculations they needed. Many of Bezos's coworkers saw no reason to spend money to change the way they stored and transmitted information. If the system is not broken, they argued, why fix it?

But for Bezos, a not-yet-broken system was not the issue. What mattered was forward thinking, anticipating the future, and being the first one there. He could foresee the day when PCs would be on every desk in every office. He needed to invent ways those small computers could handle the business needs of the next decade. That would not happen very fast at Bankers Trust.

D. E. SHAW

Bezos wanted out of banking and into what he called "second-phase automation." Computers and other electronic technology were being used to make many business processes automatic. This was "first-phase automation." It was simply using tools to do things faster or better. Technology could calculate formulas, rearrange information, print names on envelopes, or read a bar code on a grocery item. All these tasks were first-phase automation. This type of automation was electronic evolution, a logical chain of progress. Second-phase automation would use technology to do things that had never been done before. Instead of calculating formulas, it could decide what formula should be used. Instead of rearranging information, it could ferret out new data. Rather than printing names, second-phase automation could determine which names needed to receive what information. Second-phase automation would not be evolution; it would be revolution. And Bezos wanted to be at the center of any revolution.

He got his chance at D. E. Shaw and Company. This was a hedge fund business. It traded shares of stock on the stock market. It bought shares when and where they were cheap and sold them when and where their value was higher. Most hedge fund companies used computers to tell them what the prices of shares were at different times and places. D. E. Shaw was different. It programmed computers to understand how the stock market worked and let the computers pick which stocks to buy and sell. After two years at Bankers Trust, Bezos applied for a job with this revolutionary firm.

The man who interviewed him recognized that Bezos was intelligent, hardworking, creative, logical, and very good with computers. He recommended that his boss, David Shaw, hire him, saying prophetically, "He's going to make someone a lot of money someday."[2]

Even though he started at D. E. Shaw as a vice president, Bezos referred to himself as an "in-house geek."[3] Within two years, however, he had risen to become the company's youngest senior vice president. He did make a lot of money for the firm. He also made a lot for himself. He earned more than a million dollars a year.[4] And the job was fun.

JEFF AND MACKENZIE

Working at D. E. Shaw was a good career move for Bezos. It was a good personal move, too. When he started there in 1990, he was a bachelor and almost twenty-seven years old. He had approached finding a wife in the same logical, analytical way he looked at everything. He had a plan. He asked his friends to set him up on blind dates, and he listed the qualifications for the girls he would date. He wanted someone as hardworking, creative, and fun loving as he was. He told them he was looking for a wife who was clever enough to figure out how to get him out of a prison in a third world country. (Not that he

MacKenzie Bezos, Author

Even when she was a child, MacKenzie Bezos wanted to be a writer. Her creative writing teacher in college was Toni Morrison, the Nobel Prize–winning novelist. MacKenzie worked for her as a research assistant.

When MacKenzie decided to write a book of her own, it took her eight years. She reworked it so many times she said it was like writing three or four novels. Finally, in 2005, she published *The Testing of Luther Albright*. It received good reviews.

ever planned to be in a prison!) He wanted a wife who, like him, did not let obstacles stop her. His dating plan did not work, but he did find the woman he wanted to marry. He found her at D. E. Shaw.

MacKenzie Tuttle met all his qualifications. She was a hard worker. At Shaw, she was employed as a researcher. She was creative; she wrote fiction stories. She was also smart. Like Jeff, she had graduated from Princeton, but six years after he did. And she proved at their wedding that she loved having fun. Their reception included a time for all the guests to play games. Not quiet table games, but wild outdoor games that got everyone soaked with water balloons.

A pleasant family life and a good job did not settle Bezos. The entrepreneur in him kept searching for new avenues to explore. Fortunately, D. E. Shaw gave him the opportunity to do just that. The company was making money. David Shaw wanted to find or create new businesses in which to invest that money. He assigned Bezos the task of looking for business possibilities in an obscure technology that was just beginning. It was called the Internet.

OPPORTUNITY KNOCKS

At the beginning of the 1990s, few people had heard of the Internet, even though the technology for an interconnected system of computers had been around since the late 1960s. During that era, a forerunner to the Internet known as the ARPANET was developed for military communication in the event of an emergency. The U.S. Department of Defense feared that a nuclear attack or natural disaster could destroy phone lines. So the agency invented a way to pass vital information between computers connected by special telecommunications lines.

The main ARPANET computers were housed in four universities, but before long, other universities were hooked up, too. In the

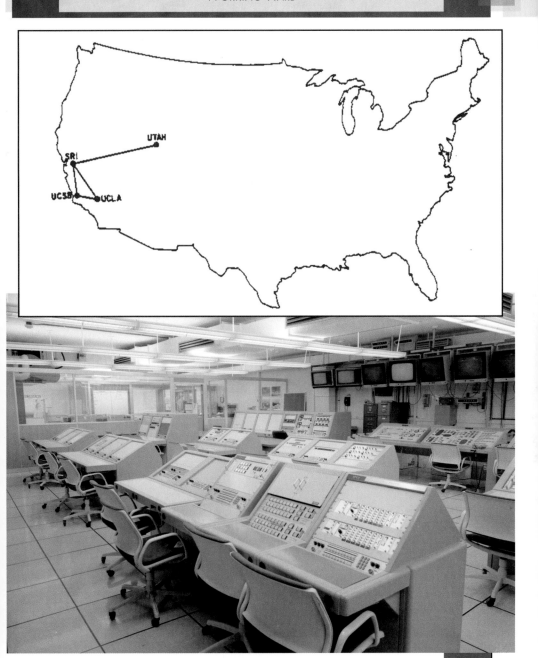

Computers connected to an ARPANET station *(bottom)* transmitted electronic information "packets" to other computers at four universities in the western United States *(top)*. The schools involved were the University of California at Los Angeles (UCLA), the Stanford Research Institute (SRI) at Stanford University, the University of California at Santa Barbara (UCSB), and the University of Utah. Today's Internet spans the entire globe.

1970s, science and engineering students took advantage of the system to communicate about their research, much in the same way we now use electronic mail, or e-mail. However, because the government built and owned the technology, its use in the early years was restricted to research, education, and government.

By 1990, the Internet system was still rather cumbersome. Very few computers were connected to other computers outside office or company networks. And, in addition, the information that could be found on the Internet was not interesting to the vast majority of ordinary people.

All that began to change around 1993. That year, technological advances began to make the Internet easier to navigate. First, hyperlinks, which had been around for years, became more widespread. Hyperlinks are words or pictures that can connect one computer to another with a simple click. Hyperlink technology—basically the ability to "point and click"—linked Internet users in dozens of countries. The matrix of interconnections became known as the World Wide Web.

A second development that accelerated the use of the Internet was an invention by a group of students at the University of Illinois. They created a Web browser that made it easy to explore and use the World Wide Web. Called Mosaic, the browser used graphics instead of text to locate information. With Mosaic, anyone with a mouse could find his or her way around the Web.

These creations made the Internet user-friendly to more than scientists and educators. Large corporations started to put information on their own Web sites. They gave descriptions of their companies, addresses and phone numbers, and news about their industries. No one in the early 1990s was using the Web directly to

N   C   S   A

MOSAIC

X Window System • Microsoft Windows • Macintosh

The "S" in the original logo for the Mosaic Web browser reflected the global possibilities of the World Wide Web. The NCSA acronym, above the Mosaic name, stands for the National Center for Supercomputing Applications. Software engineers at the NCSA designed the Mosaic browser. The same engineers later started their own company, which became Netscape Communications Corporation. The new company produced a better browser, Netscape Navigator, which is widely used today.

buy or sell. Some businesses listed their products, but customers had to phone or mail in orders to purchase those products. The Internet was still used strictly for the exchange of information, not the exchange of dollars for goods.

Everything was in place, however, for someone to turn the Web into a shopping mall. Personal computers were in nearly every office and in many homes in America. A large number of computer users were already connected to the Internet. Businesses were beginning to advertise their names and their products. The Web was ready to reach its potential.

THE IDEA

Bezos the entrepreneur was the right person in the right place at the right time. He was somewhat familiar with the Internet. At Princeton, he was one of the techies who had used the medium for research. He had been introduced to it in an astrophysics class. His degree was in computer science, and working with computers was his passion.

In 1994, just as the Internet was taking off, his boss gave him the job of looking on the Web for new business opportunities. As he searched the Web that spring, Bezos uncovered a startling

statistic. More and more people were using the
Web, or "logging on." Web usage was growing
at a phenomenal rate of 2,300 percent a year. It
was nearly impossible to calculate the huge number of people that figure represented. But the
government was in the process of opening up the
Web to private enterprise, allowing companies
to use it for electronic buying and selling, or
e-commerce. That meant that each one of those
users could become a customer of some business.
Bezos wanted first crack at operating that
business. "We can be a complete first mover in
e-commerce," he speculated.[5]

But what kind of business would work?
What product would lots of people buy? What
kind of item would they purchase without seeing
or handling it? It would have to be a common
item, and it would need to be easy to ship long
distances.

Bezos started by examining mail-order
companies. Their customers bought everyday
merchandise from catalogs. In no time, Bezos
compiled a list of twenty different kinds of mail-
order products that met his criteria. They included
clothing, office supplies, computer software, music,
and books.

In his careful, methodical way, Bezos analyzed each product category. One stood out as clearly superior. He ticked off the advantages. For one, sales in the industry had been growing at a decent pace every year. Second, no single company had a monopoly, so there would be no strong competition, at least at first. Third, the many companies that sold the items had computerized lists of their inventories, so part of the work of setting up an online business was already done. Finally, there were more than three million products on the market, enough to satisfy every taste. And three million was too many to list in a catalog, but every one could be recorded on the Web. He had no doubt; the first e-commerce business had to be a bookstore.

As luck would have it, when Bezos came to this conclusion, he had a golden opportunity to learn about the book business. The American Booksellers Association was just about to begin its annual convention. Wasting no time, Bezos flew from New York to Los Angeles to attend the convention. He talked with the people who supplied books to retail stores, and the more he learned about how they operated, the more convinced he became that an Internet bookstore would work.

JEFF BEZOS TRIVIA

Named his golden retriever Kamala after a metamorph in an episode of *Star Trek: The Next Generation*.

Buys about ten books a month.

Favorite novel: *The Remains of the Day*, by Kazuo Ishiguro, a character study of an English butler reminiscing about his thirty years of service.

Nearly always dresses in the same "uniform": khaki slacks and light blue button-down shirt, open at the collar.

Heroes: Thomas Edison, a brilliant innovator; and Walt Disney, a visionary.

Time magazine's 1999 Person of the Year.

Bezos poses at Amazon.com's headquarters. The company occupies 186,000 square feet of office space in the sixteen-story PacMed Building, located on Beacon Hill in Seattle. From their offices, Bezos and his employees enjoy impressive views of the Olympic and Cascade mountain ranges, Mount Rainier, Elliott Bay, and downtown Seattle.

The booksellers supplied hundreds of brick-and-mortar stores—physical buildings—but he described his idea of selling even more books to even more people through an Internet store. The major book suppliers were intrigued.

But Bezos's boss was not interested. Shaw thought an online bookstore might be a good idea, but he was not willing to take the risk of doing something so drastically different. Besides, he wanted Bezos, his senior vice president, to concentrate on more profitable activities.

Bezos, however, knew that his idea was a winner. Just as he never doubted that he could connect mirrors and motors to make an infinity cube, he was certain he could link buyers and suppliers in an entirely new way of doing business. He was obsessed with the untapped possibilities of the Internet. "It was like the wild, wild West," he said. "A new frontier."[6]

THE DECISION

A frontier is a risky place. When Bezos told Shaw he wanted to quit his job and start his own business, Shaw pointed out some of the risks. D. E. Shaw was a stable, proven company; Bezos would give that up for an unknown. He would be losing his extremely high salary and living without an income for some time. There was a good chance his online bookstore would never make money. Shaw asked Bezos to reconsider.

As he did with every big decision, Bezos analyzed the risks and the potential benefits of the two choices. But his passion for computers, his excitement about his new project, and his hurry to be the first in e-commerce made his decision difficult. How could he know which was better—staying at Shaw or starting his own business? He settled on a decision-making method he called "regret minimization." He would try to minimize, or reduce, the number of things he might feel sorry about later in life. He tried to imagine all the consequences of the different choices. For each one he asked himself: When I am eighty years old, how will I feel if I make this choice and it has this result?

He thought about leaving Shaw—walking away from Wall Street, the financial industry, the big bonuses, the good salary. When he was eighty, would he regret not staying at Shaw? No, he thought. He would simply get another job. If he started a new business and it succeeded, would he regret that? Of course not. If he went ahead with his bookstore and failed miserably, would he be sorry? No, not even then. The eternal optimist, he would have been glad for the adventure, and he would find something else to do. But what if he stayed at D. E. Shaw and never tested his dream, never saw for himself what the Internet could do, never stepped into the new frontier? That, he knew, he would deeply regret.

So the decision was made. Although he had trouble convincing his boss that it was the best course of action, he had no problem with his family. MacKenzie was fully supportive. His parents were surprised but positive. They had no idea what the Internet was, but they had total faith in their son. Whatever he attempted, wherever he went, they knew he would succeed.

CHAPTER THREE

HAVING FUN

S hortly after deciding to build an online bookstore, Bezos knew he would have to move. New York and the East Coast represented old business. Some of the companies there had been around for a hundred or more years. The businesses of the future were located in the West. Apple, Microsoft, Starbucks, Costco, Eddie Bauer—all were headquartered in western states.

But where in the West? As always, Bezos analyzed the options. First he established the

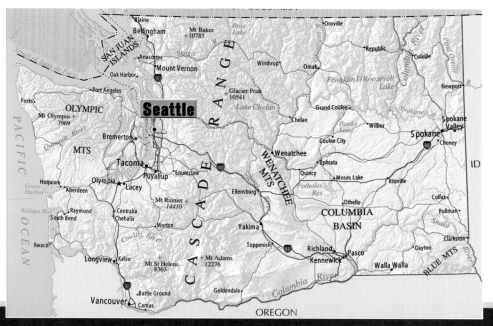

Named after a chief of the Suquamish Native American tribe, Seattle is the largest city in Washington State. Seattle, located in the Pacific Northwest, is well known as the site of Boeing Aircraft factories and the Starbucks Corporation, as well as the birthplace of grunge music.

criteria. The number-one requirement was that the city he chose would have people who knew computers. He was about to use the Web to do something that had not been done before, and he needed to hire technical geniuses who could help him make it happen. Several cities in the Silicon Valley of California were possibilities, as well as Seattle, Washington.

Which state the city was in was also important. People living in the state where the business was located would pay sales tax in addition to the cost of the merchandise; out-of-state buyers would not pay the tax. So people who lived in the same state as the business might decide to purchase their books elsewhere to avoid the tax. Bezos wanted to minimize the number of people who might make that decision, so he needed to locate in a state with a small population. That ruled out California. Of the remaining states Bezos was considering, the one with the smallest population was Colorado, then Oregon, then Nevada, and finally Washington.

The third criterion was proximity to the product. The business had to be close to a book wholesaler. A wholesaler, or distributor, bought large quantities of books from publishers and sold them in smaller quantities to bookstores. Bookstores, as retailers, sold the books to the individual customers. Bezos's company had to be close enough to a large wholesaler so his employees could get the books and ship them to their customers quickly. The biggest book distribution center in the country, Ingram, was in Roseburg, Oregon.

After narrowing the list to a few cities, Bezos studied and compared the pros and cons of each. He had a friend in one of the places on his list who sang the praises of his city. It was situated on an inlet of the Pacific Ocean where he could swim and sail. It was a short drive to snow-capped mountains with excellent skiing. As a bonus, the friend wanted to invest financially in the Internet idea. And he could connect Bezos with lawyers, realtors, bankers, and other people who would be helpful. When everything was considered, Bezos settled on his friend's city: Seattle.

THE MOVE WEST

Once he made the decision, Bezos lost no time. "When something is growing 2,300 percent a year," he said, "you have to move fast."[1] As soon as he could pack his things, he started on the 2,860-mile (4,600-kilometer) trip from New York to Seattle. At the beginning of July 1994, Jeff and MacKenzie shipped everything they owned to Jeff's friend in Seattle and then flew to Texas to visit Jeff's family. Since they did not own a car, Jeff's parents gave them a 1988 Chevrolet Blazer for their trip.

They made the move almost immediately after deciding to launch the new business. It had not been many weeks since Jeff's discovery about the exploding possibilities of the Internet, so the plan for the online bookstore was not fully formed. Jeff had a good idea of what he wanted to do, but that idea was not on paper. It needed to be written down so that people who might want to invest in it could understand this radical concept.

Jeff could not wait. He would work out the details of the plan as they traveled. He had MacKenzie drive, and he sat next to her with a laptop computer. As they talked, he typed. By the time they arrived in Seattle, the first draft of the business plan was written.

The business needed a name. Bezos liked the thought that ordering books on the Internet would be so quick and easy that it would seem like magic; you order and—abracadabra!—your book is on your doorstep. Abracadabra—that was the sense he wanted people to have about doing business with him. But it was a little long, so he shortened it to Cadabra. It was a good name, he thought.

With a plan and a name, Bezos was ready to make his business official. He had to incorporate it, which required having a lawyer fill out all the government paperwork to allow the business to operate legally. He could not wait until he arrived in Seattle. While still on the road, he called the lawyer his friend had recommended.

A NEW NAME

When Bezos said over the cell phone that he was going to call his online bookstore Cadabra, the lawyer hesitated. What the lawyer thought he heard was Cadaver. Bezos was mortified. Would people really mistake his enchanting name for a dead body? Although the company was incorporated as Cadabra on July 5, 1994, Bezos knew the name would have to be changed.

It took a few weeks to come up with just the right name. He would, of course, have to establish criteria for the name. Then he would need to analyze all the names that met the criteria. That was how he did everything.

He started with the most important requirement: It must begin with the letter "A." Just as names are listed alphabetically in the phone book, they appear in the same order on a Web search. He wanted his company to be at the top of the list. So Bezos studied the "A" section of the dictionary.

Before long, he found the perfect word. It was the name of a river in South America, a place that was exotic and different, just as his store would be. The river was the biggest in the world,[2] and his business would be the biggest store in the world. The river was not just a little larger than all others; it was ten times larger! His bookstore would not merely top the competition; it would leave all the others far behind. Yes, the name was ideal. He would call his venture Amazon.com.

SETTING UP SHOP

With a solid business plan and a great name, Bezos needed a building from which to operate. Within a week after arrival, he had found a two-bedroom house to rent. It was an older, inexpensive home in the Seattle suburb of Bellevue. It looked rather ordinary for a man who was used to a million-dollar income. But Bezos cared about only one thing. The house had to have a garage. He could have rented office space, but instead he wanted a garage. The giants of the computer age—Bill Hewlett and Dave Packard, Steve Jobs and Steve Wozniak—had created their first inventions in garages. Bezos intended to change history just as Hewlett-Packard and Apple Computers had. He wanted to be able to say his company started in a garage.

When Jeff Bezos was just starting out, he had to save money every chance he got. This picture shows him kneeling on one of the early Amazon.com desks made from a door resting on two-by-fours. His frugal approach helped Bezos position Amazon as the leader in online book sales by the time this photo was taken in December 2000.

At the time he rented the house, the room was not being used as a garage. It had been made into a recreation room. It had a linoleum floor and a large, black, potbellied stove in the middle. But it had been a garage at one time, so he could truthfully say he began Amazon.com in his garage.

The generation that would be buying from Bezos was big on image. And Bezos knew what image he wanted to create. He wanted everything about his company's start-up to look and feel humble as well as revolutionary. That meant furnishing his garage "office" as cheaply as he could. He would not need much—a desk and a couple of computer workstations. He went to a hardware store and bought three doors and some two-by-fours. From these he made a desk and two tables. Each one cost about $60 to build.

HIRING THE RIGHT PEOPLE

The physical office was not nearly as important to Bezos as the people in it. He had already decided he would work with only the best. It took him a few months, but he found just the right people. First he hired Shel Kaphan, a man who had helped start companies in the Silicon Valley of California. Second, he found Paul Barton-Davis, a British scientist at the University

Jeff Bezos made a point of bringing highly qualified people to his team. David Risher, pictured here, was hired as Amazon's senior vice president of product development. Risher, who was a class-mate of Bezos's at Princeton University, came with a lot of computer experience. Before Bezos hired him, Risher had spent six years with the Microsoft Corporation.

of Washington's Computer Science and Engineering Department. Both were computer programmers. They would write the programs that would make the online bookstore work.

While Kaphan and Barton-Davis worked on the computers, Bezos's wife, MacKenzie, handled the nontechnical jobs. She ran errands, made phone calls, and purchased whatever was needed. For the first year and a half, MacKenzie also did the bookkeeping. Bezos knew computers, and he trusted his partner to run the office.

But no one on his tiny team knew anything about selling books. So Bezos enrolled in a crash course offered by the American Booksellers Association. By November, he had pieced together a makeshift office, had assembled a crew of four people, and knew something about the book business. He was ready to begin building his company.

A NEW KIND OF STOREFRONT

Beginning an online store was not like starting any other type of retail business. Bezos had no models. Amazon.com was the first Internet retailer. Some book companies were listing some of their merchandise online, but people usually had to place their orders by phone or mail. Unlike these, Amazon would be a true retailer.

This meant Bezos would have to create a totally new kind of "storefront." The traditional retail company had a physical building. Bezos needed to build a Web site instead. He also had to figure out how he would connect with customers.

This customer is making a purchase in a traditional bookstore. Amazon.com duplicated all of the important elements of such a store: a large selection of books, gift items, featured displays, helpful clerks, and friendly service. The largest traditional bookstores carry less than 200,000 titles, but today Amazon offers more than 4.7 million titles.

People buying books had to be able to move around in his store, choose what they wanted, pay for their purchases, and receive the items they bought. This required a customer interface, or connection, that was unlike any other. The only customer interface for most computer users was e-mail. Non-techies were just beginning to learn how to use the Internet, so Bezos had to make navigating his site easy for them.

The Amazon team also had to compile a number of databases—records of products, customers, orders placed, orders in process, and orders fulfilled. Brick-and-mortar stores had inventories—tables, shelves, and stockrooms full of merchandise. Bezos had lists. Lists of books from different suppliers. Lists of books in stock and books out of stock. Lists of books in print, books out of print, and books soon to be printed. Traditional retailers had walk-in customers; Bezos would have customer identification codes. Brick-and-mortar stores had filing cabinets of customer receipts; Bezos would have electronic records. A sales clerk handed the purchased item to the buyer; Bezos had a database of customer addresses and shipping information.

The software that was available could not do what Bezos wanted. So nearly everything about the Web site, interfaces, and databases had to be created from scratch. Amazon's three-man, one-woman workforce began to build the structures the business would need in November 1994.

As Amazon.com was growing, this was one of its early offices. The building is located at 2710 First Avenue South, in Seattle. The surrounding neighborhood was not very glamorous. Bezos was not concerned with the appearance or location of his headquarters because his customers saw only his Internet site.

Some of it was slow, monotonous work. Kaphan described building the inventory database—the list of the millions of books available—as something like emptying a swimming pool with a straw.[3] But other tasks were exciting and fun. The team was constructing something that had never been made.

IN TODAY'S AMAZON OFFICE . . .

- Whiteboards line the inside walls of the building's elevators so employees can scribble whatever they want.

- Huge posters of the company's vision and core values fill the walls of distribution facilities.

- Radio Amazon broadcasts inspirational messages from Bezos.

- Every desk is made from a door.

THE ORIGINAL AMAZON OFFICE

The garage "office" where the construction was taking place presented quite a challenge. It was barely large enough for the two workstations the crew set up. To gain more room, Bezos took out the potbellied stove. To continue working through the cold Seattle winter, he installed two small space heaters. The room did not have enough outlets to power all the computers, much less the lights and the heaters. Extension cords ran to the garage from several rooms in the house. Still there was not always enough electricity.

The office had absolutely no room for meetings. So when any face-to-face business was conducted, Bezos had to get together with clients elsewhere. He found the perfect place about a mile from his home. It was a Starbucks cafe that was inside a Barnes & Noble bookstore. There, in their competitor's store, Bezos, Kaphan, and Barton-Davis met often to plan and solve problems. That is where MacKenzie signed contracts with the freight companies that would deliver Amazon's books.

BUILDING THE BUSINESS

Before the first book could be delivered, the foundation of the business had to be laid. This, of course, took time. Developing the software, testing programs, working out deals with suppliers and shippers—the preparation stage took a full six months. Building the foundation also required money. The office, the equipment, the people— nothing was free. For the first six months, Bezos paid for everything. But during that time he was not making any money, and his savings were rapidly dwindling.

To keep going, he sold shares of Amazon stock to his parents. The stock was not yet profitable, but Mike and Jackie knew that someday it would be. They knew Jeff's drive, his determination to triumph over any obstacle, and his remarkable creativity. They trusted his business instincts. "We didn't invest in Amazon," Jackie said later. "We invested in Jeff."[4]

They counted on Jeff's analytical personality. He would not pour so much of his time and money into an enterprise unless he had weighed all the possibilities for success or failure. Actually, Bezos had calculated the pros and cons of this venture and decided it was more likely to fail than succeed. He figured that the average Internet company had a 10 percent chance of making it. Because he had hired superb talent and had a great business plan, and because he was ever the optimist, Bezos thought his chance of succeeding was higher—maybe 30 percent. So he told his parents not to invest, not to buy stock in Amazon, unless they were prepared to lose their money.[5] They invested $300,000 in their son's idea.

Despite the odds against him, Bezos did not intend to lose that money. In the spring of 1995, he began to beta test his electronic store. He set up a dummy Web site and invited three hundred people to act as shoppers. They were to go to the mock site, look around and order books as though the site were real, and report back on their

experience. The Amazon team would then correct
any problems. Bezos asked the beta testers to keep
the operation secret.

Welcome to Amazon.com Books!

One million titles,
consistently low prices.

(If you explore just one thing, make it our personal notification service. We think it's very cool!)

SPOTLIGHT! -- AUGUST 16TH
These are the books we love, offered at Amazon.com low prices. The spotlight moves **EVERY**
day so please come often.

ONE MILLION TITLES
Search Amazon.com's million title catalog by author, subject, title, keyword, and more... Or take
a look at the books we recommend in over 20 categories... Check out our customer reviews and
the award winners from the Hugo and Nebula to the Pulitzer and Nobel... and bestsellers are
30% off the publishers list...

EYES & EDITORS, A PERSONAL NOTIFICATION SERVICE
Like to know when that book you want comes out in paperback or when your favorite author
releases a new title? Eyes, our tireless, automated search agent, will send you mail. Meanwhile,
our human editors are busy previewing galleys and reading advance reviews. They can let you
know when especially wonderful works are published in particular genres or subject areas. Come
in, meet Eyes, and have it all explained.

YOUR ACCOUNT
Check the status of your orders or change the email address and password you have on file with
us. Please note that you **do not** need an account to use the store. The first time you place an
order, you will be given the opportunity to create an account.

Amazon.com's first home page was very simple. The only picture
was the company logo. Users navigated the site by clicking on
hyperlinks, seen here as underlined blue words. Hyperlinks allowed
customers to quickly view lists of book titles, best-sellers, Amazon
recommendations, book reviews, and their personal accounts.

GOING LIVE

By July 16, 1995, all the bugs had been worked out, and Bezos was confident that Amazon was ready. So without any fanfare or big announcement, he "went live," putting the real Web site online. It was not very fancy. It was mostly text with one graphic: a winding river splitting a blue, triangular block so as to form the letter "A." Beneath the A were the words "Amazon.com: Earth's biggest bookstore." The page boasted one million titles. Bezos did not advertise the site's debut. He simply e-mailed his three hundred beta testers, told them the store was open for business, and asked them to tell their friends.

The team expected a slow start. To keep up everyone's enthusiasm, Barton-Davis rigged the computers to give off a bell sound when an order came in. At first, the bell went off five or six times a day. Every time they heard it, the staff cheered. Before the first week ended, however, the bell rang so often its sound had to be shut off. In the first week, sales totaled $12,438. In the second week, the figure was $14,792. In the first month, Amazon shipped books to paying customers in all fifty states and forty-five foreign countries.[6]

The company's immediate success was probably due to two factors. One was that the people using the Internet then were mostly "early adopters." These were the people who were first to try new things. They were the ones who had cell phones, satellite dishes, and other electronic gadgets before such items were popular. They were not afraid to purchase things online. They were eager to check out this new way of doing business. And once they tried it, they liked it.

The other factor Bezos would later call luck. Just three days after his site appeared on the Web, he received an e-mail from another new online company called Yahoo!. The Yahoo! people liked the Amazon site and wanted to include it on Yahoo!'s "What's Cool" feature. Since more people visited Yahoo! than any other Web site, Amazon's appearance there gave it great exposure.

Another bit of luck came before the store was a year old. On May 16, 1996, the *Wall Street Journal* ran a front-page story on Bezos and Amazon.com. It painted a portrait of the novel bookstore as an exciting, growing, trendy place. The story reached beyond the early adopters to a new pool of potential book buyers. Overnight, sales doubled. And they kept climbing.

GROWING PAINS

But the phenomenal success brought problems. For one thing, the small Amazon staff was not prepared to fill so many orders. Bezos had hired programmers, not packing and shipping clerks, and the books had to be mailed to the people who bought them. So at the beginning, everyone, including Jeff and MacKenzie, pitched in. They often stayed until midnight, wrapping packages in the crowded office.

Before long, the office was not large enough for the growing number of computers, people, and packing crates. Bezos moved his operation out of his garage to a commercial building. But in a matter of months, that facility was too small also. He outgrew a third building in five more months. In Amazon's first three years, the business moved four times to five different locations.

Space was a small problem compared to money. Starting the business had been very costly. Orders were pouring in, but it would take thousands of sales just to make up for what had already been spent. In 1995, in its first six months, Amazon.com lost $303,000. And Bezos had no money left. If he was to keep going, he needed to find people who would invest in his company.

That was no easy task. Not only was the company new, but the whole idea of selling products on the Internet was still unproven. Sure, the number of people buying was surprising everyone, but would the good times continue? What would happen when the novelty wore off?

GET BIG FAST

Bezos's business plan was radically unlike any that was known to work. The goal of most businesses was to make a profit as quickly as possible. Not so with Amazon. Bezos's stated goal was to get big fast. He thought it was more important to grow the company quickly, to corner the market, and develop his Internet bookstore before anyone else figured out how. Bezos consciously chose to put his resources into getting big fast instead of making money. He often said that he was postponing profits in order to change the world.

He told potential investors he did not expect to make a profit for the first two years. He just had to convince them that his plan would eventually make money for them. In the end, it was not his plan, but Bezos himself that convinced them. His supreme confidence in what he was creating, his genuine enthusiasm in what it would do for the customer, and his irrepressible optimism won over about twenty investors. By the end of 1995, he had secured almost $1 million in financial backing.

As expected, Amazon.com did not make a profit in its first two years. And Bezos had spent the investment money. He had spent far more from his personal funds and his family's contributions. In fact, by April 1997, Amazon had lost a total of $9 million.

But Bezos was not discouraged. Instead of looking at the losses, he focused on the gains. In the first three months of 1997, sales totaled $16 million, more than for all twelve months of the year before. Eighty thousand people were visiting the Web site every day. He had 340,000 customers, and the name Amazon.com was known in a hundred countries. Everything was growing by leaps and bounds. In fact, his company was getting big even faster than he had planned. He needed to keep the momentum going. He could concentrate on making a profit later.

AMAZON.COM GOES PUBLIC

To secure the money that would allow him to keep the momentum going, Bezos wanted

SOME AMAZON.COM FIRSTS

October 1995—First 100-order day

Before October 1996—First 100-order hour

October 1997—First online retailer to serve one million customers

Before July 2000—First 100-order minute

Amazon.com to become a public company. This means that he would allow the general public to buy shares in Amazon. The shares would be traded—bought and sold—on the stock market. He would not have to find new investors. Everyone who wanted to own a piece of the company could buy stock in it. For the initial public offering—the company's first sale of stock to the public—Bezos would decide how many shares he would sell and how much each would cost. After the company went public, the price of the shares would rise or fall depending on how much people were willing to pay for them.

Three days before Amazon was scheduled to go public, a bookstore war threatened Bezos's carefully crafted plan. Barnes & Noble, the largest bookseller in the country, launched a two-pronged attack. First, it announced that it was going into the online business with its own Web

Joy Covey (center) was Amazon.com's chief financial officer from 1996 to 2000. Here, she visits the Chicago Board Options Exchange, a type of stock market. Two executives of the exchange, Thomas Ascher (left) and William Brodsky, explain how to use equipment that will help Covey follow the activity of Amazon stock. The price of the company's stock rises and falls as it is traded throughout the day.

site. It touted the site as the premier place for book lovers and book buyers everywhere. Second, it sued Amazon. The suit charged that Amazon's claim to be "Earth's biggest bookstore" was false because the Internet company was technically not a store.

One influential writer watched the war unfold and declared that Amazon.com would soon be Amazon.toast. Another called it Amazon.bomb. They assumed the competition from the giant retailer would bury the upstart dot-com. But Bezos, in his characteristically optimistic manner, saw the battle as great fun. Barnes & Noble's attack was proof that Amazon was taking a significant amount of business away from the biggest bookstore in America.

Invigorated by the challenge, Bezos took Amazon public on May 15, 1997. He sold off 10 percent of the company. His parents, brother, and sister together already owned 10 percent, and he kept 42 percent for himself. The remaining 38 percent was owned by the earlier investors. Even though only 10 percent of the company was sold in the initial public offering, that 10 percent brought Amazon.com an additional $54 million.[7]

It was not enough to make a profit, but it was enough to keep growing, to stay in front, and that is exactly what Bezos intended to do. He had already proven that e-commerce was where business was headed. He had already made history. Now he intended to make his company the model for e-trade to be followed by future generations of e-tailers.

CHAPTER FOUR

SETTING THE STANDARDS

I n traditional commerce, there is a widely recognized set of standard business practices. One must follow these standards in order to achieve success. But there were no established guidelines for Bezos to follow. Because he was first in e-commerce, he set the standards for the industry. And because he was phenomenally successful, others followed his lead. The standards for Amazon.com, the fundamental principles that make it work so well, are the company's six core values: customer obsession, ownership, bias for action, frugality, high hiring bar, and innovation. The walls of every Amazon building are plastered with posters reminding employees of these six values. Bezos will not let his workers forget that these are the foundation of the company.

CUSTOMER OBSESSION

Bezos is obsessed with his customers. Posted even bigger than the six core values is Amazon's vision: To be the world's most customer-centric company. Every decision in the company is based on the supreme importance of the customer. The reason any retailer stays in business is the customer. From the very beginning, Bezos determined that everything he did at Amazon would be done to make the customer happy.

Bezos wanted Amazon's customer obsession to go beyond friendly service and generous return policies. He wanted it to be about seeing things from the point of view of the shopper. Bezos knew that people often went to a physical bookstore not just for a book but for a pleasurable experience. He wanted to give his customers an even better experience in his online store. So he worked to take a visit to a brick-and-mortar store and translate it to the Web. In his typically

Jane Radke Slade, shown here in 1999, when she was Amazon.com's director of customer services. Under her watchful eye, Amazon employees helped customers find items and assisted them if they had problems with their orders. Then as now, many issues related to customer service were settled through e-mail communication.

SOME INTERESTING AMAZON ORDERS

The first book sold was *Fluid Concepts and Creative Analogies: Computer Models of the Fundamental Mechanisms of Thought* by Douglas Hofstadter.

In August 1996, a customer ordered twelve books, all with the name Marsha in the title.

The one millionth customer bought *Windows NT: An Administrator's Bible* and *The Royals* by Kitty Kelly.

Amazon sent 2,000 books to a charity that built a library in the African nation of Zambia.

On the company's tenth anniversary, July 16, 2005, *Harry Potter and the Half-Blood Prince* (Book 6) was released. Amazon made more money on the sale of that book on that day than on all books in the entire first year in business.

methodical fashion, he thought through everything people would see and do from the moment they walked into a store until they walked out with a purchase. Then he duplicated those experiences in his cyberstore.

First, brick-and-mortar bookstore customers usually pass tables of featured items—best-sellers, seasonal specials, gift suggestions. That was easy for the techies at Amazon to re-create. From the very beginning of the Web site, a "Spotlight" feature highlighted different books. As the technology became better, more books and other items were featured on Amazon's opening page. The selections changed daily.

Some shoppers go directly to the section of the store that displays the types of books that interest them. Others walk up and down the aisles, waiting for something to catch their attention. Amazon could provide both experiences online. Books were cataloged by title, author, and subject, so the site could take the focused customer directly to a particular book. A list of more than one million titles allowed browsers to look for as long as they liked.

Bookstore customers often read a book's blurbs—the short bits of praise that traditionally are printed on a book's dust jacket. Or they might skim through a few pages to see if it is a book they want to buy. So Bezos also posted blurbs. He even hired people to write blurbs for books that did not have one. And before long, Amazon introduced its own "Look Inside the Book" feature, which let online shoppers read parts of a book before deciding to purchase it.

amazon.com.

Dear Amazon.com Customers,

Starting today, you can find books at Amazon.com based on *every word* inside them, not just on matches to author or title keywords. Search Inside the Book -- the name of this new feature -- searches the complete inside text of more than 120,000 books -- all 33 million pages of them. And since we've integrated Search Inside the Book into our standard search, using it is as easy as entering a search term in our regular search box.

As just one example, by searching on the term "Resistojet" I've been able to find books that I could not have found otherwise. I encourage you to try Search Inside the Book for yourself to see how powerful this new feature is.

We'd love to hear about your experiences using Search Inside the Book. We're running a contest where we'll award our grand prize winner a Segway Human Transporter. Ten additional customers will each win a $100 Amazon.com gift certificate. Visit our How It Works page to enter the contest, learn more about this new feature, and see more sample searches.

We're working hard to make your shopping experience better and to make Amazon.com the best place on the planet to find, discover and buy books. Thank you very much for being a customer.

On behalf of Amazon.com,

Jeff Bezos
Founder & CEO

On October 23, 2003, Amazon.com announced one of its new features: Search Inside the Book. Since then, improved technology has made it even easier for Amazon customers to search for specific words or phrases in a book. Within five days of this announcement, sales for books that users could "search inside" increased 9 percent.

Deciding to purchase is not always easy. Bookstore customers sometimes pick up a few books and then change their minds about some or all of them. For this reason, Amazon created the online shopping basket, so people could move around in the Internet store, placing items in and out of the basket before heading to the checkout. Unlike at traditional bookstores, at Amazon there

Amazon's Seattle distribution warehouse was a busy place ten days before Christmas 1999. During the holiday season that year, about 42 percent of all Web shoppers bought from Amazon.com. Toys, electronics, and, of course, books were top sellers. The company had to hire extra workers for the warehouse in order to ship all the orders in time for the holidays.

was no checkout line, no long wait. And for a repeat customer whose information was already on file, the transaction could be completed in one second with a single click.

At some point, the shopper might want to ask a question. Where would I find information about turtles? What age range is this book for? When will a favorite author's newest book be available? Sometimes a store clerk or manager could answer such questions, sometimes not. Amazon's team of customer service representatives could answer nearly every one through e-mail.

Using high-tech resources such as e-mail and huge databases, Bezos tried to give his cyberbusiness the feel of an old-fashioned, small-town store—the kind of store where the clerk knew his customers and remembered what they liked to read. Very few bookstores could do that in the 1990s. But Amazon could welcome visitors by name, store information about their every purchase, and recommend new items similar to ones they bought previously.

In many respects, the Amazon experience was even better than a trip to a physical bookstore. The store was open twenty-four hours a day, seven days a week. It had no parking problems. The selection was unlimited. And the laws of

TEN-YEAR GROWTH OF AMAZON.COM

Year	Number of Customers	Sales (dollars)	Profit/Loss (dollars)
1995	unavailable	511,000	−303,000
1996	180,000	15,700,000	−5,800,000
1997	1,510,000	147,800,000	−31,000,000
1998	6,200,000	610,000,000	−124,550,000
1999	14,000,000	1,640,000,000	−720,000,000
2000	20,000,000	2,760,000,000	−1,410,000,000
2001	25,000,000	3,120,000,000	−567,000,000
2002	31,000,000	3,930,000,000	−149,000,000
2003	40,000,000	5,650,000,000	+35,300,000
2004	45,000,000	6,920,000,000	+588,000,000

supply and demand allowed Bezos to keep the prices low.

OWNERSHIP

While price for the customer was going down, the value of Amazon stock was going up. Long before the company made a profit, confident investors continued to pay relatively high prices for Amazon shares. As with most stocks, the price bounced up and down. But, for Amazon, the trend was generally up. Many people wanted to own the shares.

Owning shares of Amazon meant owning part of the company. Bezos thought his employees should be part-owners, even if the "part" was very small. So some of the pay he gave his workers was in stock options. These options gave employees the right to purchase Amazon stock at a set price for a limited time. It was a little risky because the value of the stock could go down. But Bezos, the eternal optimist, believed any dip in stock price was only temporary. Owning shares in the company could make his employees rich.

Ownership in the company also tied the employees' well-being to that of Amazon. If

Amazon did well, the employees did well. If Amazon suffered, the employees made less money. Ownership was more than a psychological boost. It was a powerful motivation to work long and hard to make the company succeed.

And work hard they did, especially at the beginning. When the first floods of orders surprised everyone, people worked ten- to eighteen-hour days, seven days a week. Bezos was right there with them, working just as hard. One employee said it was "like being on a rocket ship and just holding on for dear life." But, she added, "It was fun."[1]

Bezos made sure that it was fun. True to his motto—work hard, have fun, make history— he kept work fresh and exciting with crazy contests and generous prizes. He had water pistols in his office and was known to start rubber-band wars in the warehouse. His distinct, explosive laugh echoed often through Amazon's hallways. When demands were especially heavy, he closed up shop for two-hour lunches. He put on picnics, parties, and other events. When he asked people to work beyond their typical fifty-hour workweek, he rewarded them financially. He wanted them not only to own the company but to be glad they did.

BIAS FOR ACTION

Bezos also wanted his employees to be people of action. If Amazon was to make history, its people had to think up and perform history-making acts. Creating a completely new way to do business was only the opening act. Many more would need to follow. The evolution of Amazon.com was not a series of ideas but a succession of bold actions based on those ideas. One of the first was a complete revamp of the business plan.

Bezos's original thought was to operate a Web site and outsource everything else. In other words, he would concentrate on the computer end of the business and he would use sources outside Amazon to stock and ship the books. But within the first few months, Bezos realized that his plan was impractical. Orders were streaming in, and submitting a request once a day to book distributors was slowing down delivery to the customer. So, based on the number-one value of customer obsession, Bezos decided Amazon needed to stock books in its own warehouse. In November 1996, he leased the first of what would eventually become a network of six warehouses. These were strategically placed around the country so that no customer was far from Amazon's products.

Bezos's next big action was a move from "Earth's Biggest Bookstore" to "Earth's Biggest Everything Store." Almost as soon as the site went online, customers began e-mailing, asking Amazon to carry videos and music. It was a logical next step. All along, Bezos had envisioned his company as more than just a place to buy books. His passion was not books but revolutionizing people's lives through computer technology. Books just happened to be the easiest thing to sell with that technology. They were merely the starting point. In June 1998, just a year after going public, Amazon added CDs, videos, and DVDs to its offerings. The tagline above its name now read "Books, Music & More."

The decision to expand to additional products was driven by the goal of serving the customer. But it was also based on sound analysis. For all his just-do-it optimism, Bezos analyzed every action he considered. He studied the numbers. "The best kinds of decisions," he insisted, are "fact-based decisions."[2] The fact was that adding new products would bring in money without costing much. Amazon already had millions of customers. It had systems for processing and delivering purchases. Selling new types of items to existing customers through existing systems made economic sense.

The addition of new products was so successful that during the 2004 Christmas season, customers bought more electronics than books. In 2000, Amazon's logo had a smile (for the importance of pleasing the customer) that pointed from the A in its name to the Z. It said, "Amazon.com and you're done."

Bezos, of course, was not done. His bias for action meant that he was never finished. He was always looking for ways to expand, to improve, to give the customer a better experience. At its tenth anniversary, in July 2005, Amazon carried thirty-one different categories of products.

Adding products was only one type of action. Another was expanding to new markets. By its ten-year anniversary, Amazon had launched Web sites registered in seven countries. The company was well on its way to being what Bezos always called it: Earth's Biggest Selection.

But it could not offer the biggest selection simply through direct sales. It would have to go to third-party selling. Amazon (the first party) would connect the customer (the second party) with a third party, which had merchandise for sale. Bezos did this in three ways. First, he built an associate's program, which linked small Web sites to Amazon. This let the littler company promote its product while Amazon handled the sale and delivery. Second, he started an auction through which individuals could advertise and sell their personal wares. Third, he formed partnerships with some of the best-known brick-and-mortar stores, allowing them to have a "store" on his site and turning the Amazon site into an Internet mall.

FRUGALITY

Bezos did all this with as little money as possible. Frugality was one of his company's core values. Like the other values, it was an outgrowth of customer obsession. He did not want to spend money on anything that did not have a direct benefit for the customer. If the customer does not see it, he figured, it should be cheap. So Amazon offices do not have expensive bookcases or high-priced artwork. To reinforce this value with all employees, every desk is, like his original, made out of a door and sawed-off two-by-fours. All other furniture, at least at the beginning, was bought at garage sales or auctions.

Although nothing is wasted on office decorating, plenty of money is spent connecting the name Amazon.com with exceptional customer service in the minds of the public. In 1997, when Amazon was close to becoming the first e-tailer to serve a million people, Bezos announced a contest to see who would be the one millionth new customer. He called it "You're One in a Million." The winner would receive a $10,000 prize, and Bezos promised to personally deliver the lucky person's order. Every day of the two-week promotion, he awarded Amazon.com T-shirts to a hundred customers. When the company reached the milestone, Bezos flew to Japan to make good on his word.

HIGH HIRING BAR

Bezos thought that money used to promote Amazon.com was money well spent. The other place he believed in spending money was on top-notch employees. He was doing something that had never been done, and he could do it only with the most talented, creative people. Fortunately for him, those were the types of people who were attracted to Amazon. Those

In 1997, Bezos flew to Japan to personally deliver an order to the man who opened Amazon.com's one millionth new-customer account. Every Amazon employee signed the packing box. Publicity stunts like this kept Amazon in the public eye, even as the company was losing tens of millions of dollars.

were the types he hired, even in the customer service department.

In many companies, customer service representatives did little more than answer the phone. At Amazon, customer service was the backbone of the company. After the programmers who created the systems and software, the customer service people were the most important employees. To be hired by Jeff Bezos for customer service, a person had to have a college degree. The person had to be able to work miracles with computers and understand the bookselling and book distribution business. He or she had to be able to figure out what book a shopper wanted from the barest information. Moreover, the first customer service representatives stepped into a system that was still a work in progress. Because of this, they often had to act as if they knew all the answers, even when there were no answers. Amazon.com's public image was very important, especially in the beginning. So Bezos could not afford to let his company develop a reputation as unorganized or chaotic. In light of all this, customer service employees had to be special people, capable, friendly, and quick-thinking. Ultimately, Amazon's customer service team succeeded in taking the faceless experience of shopping on a computer and making it personal.

Bezos paid scrupulous attention to these first five company values—customer obsession, ownership, bias for action, frugality, and a high hiring bar. All contributed in major ways to Amazon's

Amazon.com opened a distribution center in McDonough, Georgia, in 1999. The facility announced plans to hire 500 new employees, attracting applicants from all over the country. In this picture, Amazon employee Eric Knapp entertains people as they fill out their applications. He shouted trivia questions about the company and awarded Amazon.com T-shirts and hats for correct answers.

success. But many companies in all different sorts of businesses strive to abide by these same business ideals. What set Amazon apart? What allowed Jeff Bezos to make history? The answer was Amazon's innovation, its ability to succeed while doing things in new and different ways.

CHAPTER FIVE

MAKING HISTORY

Bezos hired creative people because innovation was part of who Bezos was. In the fast-moving world of e-business, coming up with new ideas was the only way to stay ahead of the pack. And no one came up with fresher ideas than Bezos and his employees. Bezos encouraged his staff to think creatively. He put them in groups and asked them to devise ways to make things work better. He thought small groups worked best for this—no more than five to seven people. No bigger, he said, than could

Some Unique Amazon Events

1999—The Amazon.com auction feature was launched with a charity auction, raising money for the preservation of the Amazon rain forest. One of the items sold was Bezos's first door desk, purchased for $30,100 by Bezos's mother, Jackie Gise.

1999—Bezos personally delivered an order to Amazon's ten millionth customer—golf clubs to a man in Boston.

2003—Bezos played tennis with Anna Kournikova at Grand Central Terminal, in New York City, for charity and to publicize a new Kournikova item on Amazon.

be fed with two pizzas. Dozens of two-pizza teams created innovations over the years. These are what kept Amazon the leader in Internet commerce.

Most of the innovations are common today, but they were revolutionary when Amazon introduced them. Simple procedures such as sending an e-mail to confirm an order and sending another when it was shipped were groundbreaking. No other Web site had personalized pages that welcomed the shopper and remembered previous purchases. Nor did they make recommendations based on those purchases. Bezos's teams developed the majority of the software and processes that are used today for online selling.

By the time other companies began e-tailing, Amazon was far out in front. To stay in front, however, Bezos had to give his customers reasons to remain loyal to Amazon. This was the very thing he loved doing—coming up with creative ways to serve his customers. New features tumbled from the fertile minds and high-powered computers of his techies:

- One-click shopping, which allows repeat customers to order by clicking on a single button

- Book rankings, which show the hottest-selling books, updated every twenty-four hours

- E-cards, which allow people to e-mail greeting cards free of charge

- Wish lists, which let customers list things they want from Amazon, like a bridal registry, and let visitors to the site view the list and purchase the items

- "Search Inside the Book," which lets customers look for words or phrases in books

In August 2000, Amazon.com partnered with Greenlight.com to sell new cars online. A tab on Amazon.com's Web site connected visitors to Greenlight's site. Using the site, customers could compare vehicles, select a car, and even get a loan to make the purchase. In 2001, Greenlight.com was bought by CarsDirect.com; Amazon continued the partnership with the new owner.

- Free shipping on orders of at least $25

- The Gold Box, a treasure chest icon of specials that last for only one hour

- Bottom of the Page Deals, or daily bargains

- A9, an Internet search engine

- Amazon Prime, which gives customers unlimited two-day shipping for a fee

THE AMAZON COMMUNITY

One of the greatest ways Bezos generated customer loyalty was by creating an online community. Bezos found ways of getting his customers to connect with one another and with Amazon. He invited people to write their own reviews of the books and other items they bought, and millions did. He conducted a "You Write the Story" contest. Well-known author John Updike penned the first paragraph of a mystery, "Murder Makes the Magazine," and visitors to Amazon contributed sentences and paragraphs via e-mail. Each week a winner won $1,000, and a grand-prize winner collected $100,000. Updike then wrote the last paragraph. In the six-week contest, 400,000 people sent in story parts.

In another contest, thousands wrote captions for panels of "The People's Doonesbury" comic strip drawn by Garry Trudeau. To promote *The Street Lawyer*, a book by best-selling author John Grisham, Amazon sent a contest winner to law school.

The innovative features are only part of the reason millions of customers remain loyal to Amazon. The other reasons are low prices, great selection, and dependable service. People buy from Amazon because they know and trust it. Bezos's six core values made the company not only the first to capture online customers but also the leader in keeping them. He is continuing to do what he vowed he would do when he started—make history.

BEZOS AND AMAZON MAKE HISTORY

Some people make the kind of history that is written in record books. Others make the sort of history that is seen in political or social movements. When Jeff Bezos made history, he changed the world. He altered the way millions of people in well over a hundred countries conduct business every day. Even more than changing the way people do business, he opened them up to new information, new resources, and new technologies.

When Bezos started on his mission, people were just discovering the Internet. But before long, Amazon.com had helped introduce hundreds of thousands of ordinary citizens to the online world. In fact, some people bought computers just to purchase books from Amazon. Bezos's customer service technicians received phone calls from dozens of people asking how to plug in a mouse so they could connect to his Web site. The techs taught them not only how to use the Amazon site but also how to understand and navigate the World Wide Web.

Bezos made history in the corporate world also. Amazon.com was a revolutionary business model. It was new not only because it was the first e-commerce model, but also because it defied all accepted business principles. Before Bezos started Amazon, the idea of "get big fast," of deferring profit for the sake of growth, was unthinkable. The concept was not taught in any business school. "It's a more patient approach," Bezos explained, "but we think it leads to a stronger, healthier company."[1] And in many ways he was right. His model proved wildly successful.

When others either tried to copy or compete with Bezos's model, he did not mind. He wanted to be first, but he did not expect to be the only e-tailer. He often said that he welcomed the competition. When the first serious competitor entered the online market (Barnes & Noble in 1997), Bezos did not try to crush the rival with aggressive marketing or cutthroat practices. Instead, he quietly developed a new feature that he hoped would make customers choose Amazon: he added an "out-of-print" department that helped shoppers find books that were no longer being published. His response to competition was to remain focused on his customers. "We pay attention to competitors," he admits, "but we obsess over customers."[2]

Bezos has even helped create some of his competition. He has permitted more than 50,000 people to download software kits his programmers developed. This has enabled others to use Amazon's technology to build their own Web sites and grow their own companies. "Our premise," he explains, "is there are going to be a lot of winners. It's not winner take all. Other people do not have to lose for us to win."[3]

BUMPS IN THE ROAD

Bezos has not won at everything he has attempted. Because of the success of Amazon and some other online retailers, a number of small online companies sprang up in what was known as the dot-com craze. In 1999, Amazon began investing in a number of these new companies, Pets.com, Living.com, Homegrocer.com, and Kozmo.com among them. When these companies collapsed in 2000, marking the so-called dot-com crash, Bezos lost money on several of his investments.

By the middle of 2001, Amazon.com's distribution center in McDonough, Georgia, was deserted. Amazon had opened the 800,000-square-foot facility less than two years earlier. After the dot-com crash, however, the company was forced to tighten its belt. All 442 workers were laid off, as were 800 other Amazon employees around the country.

Losing money meant cutting back. When the dot-com bubble burst in 2000, Amazon was forced to lay off 150 employees. In January 2001, another 1,300 workers had to go, as two distribution centers and a customer-service center were closed. This was very distressing for Bezos. But he felt the difficulty would not last long, and he cared deeply about his employees. He placed

$2.5 million of company stock in a trust fund to be distributed in 2003 among those who were laid off. Those workers, he said, "contributed to the success of the company," and therefore, he reasoned, "as we do well, they should share in the fruits of that."[4]

TAKING CARE OF BUSINESS

By 2003, Amazon was doing well. It had begun to make a profit—its first in seven years. When asked how Amazon survived when so many others failed, Bezos answered, "Because, even in that whirlwind, we kept heads-down, focused on the customer."[5]

That is the same answer he gave when asked about the future.

Even though he is a billionaire, Jeff Bezos maintains a down-to-earth image. When he enters the Amazon headquarters to work, he wears an identification badge, just like everyone else.

He pointed to everything that had changed since he began Amazon, how everything about computing had become so much cheaper and faster than it was in 1995. What did that mean for his company? He answered with a question: "What can you do with 30 times as much disk space, 20 times as much computing power, and 30 times as much bandwidth? All right, how are you going to make customers happy with all that?"[6]

Some would say this customer obsession is the reason for Amazon's phenomenal success. They would be only partially right. The real reason is Jeff Bezos, the unique man who understood that customer obsession is the key. His entrepreneurial spirit provided the vision. His methodical, analytical approach gave shape to the vision. His creativity and his treatment of obstacles as welcome challenges adjusted the vision as the company moved forward. His focus, drive, and incredible optimism energized the entire venture. Anything that was lacking was made up for by his unshakable belief in himself and in his vision. He truly worked hard, had fun, and made history.

TIMELINE

January 12, 1964—	Jeff Bezos is born in Albuquerque, New Mexico.
1982—	Bezos graduates from Palmetto High School in Miami, Florida, as valedictorian.
May 1986—	Bezos graduates summa cum laude from Princeton University; begins work at Fitel.
April 1988—	Bezos begins work at Bankers Trust.
1990–1994—	Bezos works at D. E. Shaw and Co., Inc.
1993—	Bezos marries MacKenzie Tuttle.
Spring 1994—	Bezos finds Web usage growing at 2,300 percent per year.
Summer 1994—	Bezos moves to Seattle; Cadabra, Inc., is incorporated.
Fall 1994—	Bezos sets up shop in his garage.
February 9, 1995—	Amazon.com is incorporated.
Late spring 1995—	Beta testing of Amazon.com begins.
July 16, 1995—	Web site launches. In thirty days, it makes sales in fifty states and forty-five countries.

TIMELINE

May 16, 1996— *Wall Street Journal* article causes spike in Amazon.com business.

May 15, 1997— Amazon.com goes public.

June 10, 1998— Amazon.com starts selling music CDs and movie videos and DVDs.

April 1999— Amazon.com launches auction site.

2000— Internet bubble bursts.

March 2000— Bezos's son Preston is born.

2003— Amazon.com realizes first full-year profit.

December 2004— Amazon.com sets up online donation page for tsunami victims in Asia; within two weeks, donations exceed $13 million.

2005— With a personal fortune of more than $12 billion, Bezos is ranked number 41 on *Forbes* magazine's list of the world's wealthiest people.

GLOSSARY

beta test A test of a computer product conducted before the product is released commercially.

brick-and-mortar Term used to describe a retail store that operates in a physical building, possibly but not necessarily made out of bricks and mortar.

browser Computer software that lets a user find sites on the Internet.

cyber- Prefix used to refer to things having to do with the Internet.

database A set of information organized so that a computer program can quickly select specific pieces of the information.

dot-com An Internet company.

download To copy data from a main source to a second device, such as copying a file from an online service to a personal computer.

e- Prefix meaning "electronic." Used to describe various activities conducted on the Internet such as e-mail, e-trade, and e-commerce.

entrepreneur A person who has an idea for a business or venture and starts the venture.

e-tail Electronic retail operation; buying and selling goods over the Internet.

hyperlink A word or image in an electronic document that can be clicked on by a computer user to link to another place in the document or to another document or computer site.

interface Place where two different things meet and communicate with each other. A user interface, or customer interface, allows a user to communicate with a computer's operating system.

Internet A network that connects computers.

outsource To use sources outside a company to perform some of the company's functions or provide some of the company's services.

retail The selling of goods in small quantities to consumers.

Silicon Valley Nickname for an area south of San Francisco, California, where many companies that manufacture parts for electronic and computer industries are located. Many of the parts are made of silicon, a nonmetallic element.

software Computer instructions or data, such as a program. Information that is stored electronically is software whereas the devices that store and display the information are hardware.

World Wide Web A system of Internet servers using a language or formatting that lets users link from one document or file to another by clicking on hyperlinks.

FOR MORE INFORMATION

Amazon.com
1200 Twelfth Avenue, Suite 1200
Seattle, WA 98144
(206) 266-1000
Web site: http://www.amazon.com

Forbes magazine
60 Fifth Avenue
New York, NY 10011
(800) 295-0893
Web site: http://www.forbes.com

Hoover's, Inc.
5800 Airport Boulevard
Austin, TX 78752
(512) 374-4500
Web site: http://www.hoovers.com

Ingram Book Group
1 Ingram Boulevard
La Vergne, TN 37086
(800) 937-0152
Web site: http://www.ingrambook.com

Seattle Post-Intelligencer (newspaper)
101 Elliott Avenue W.
Seattle, WA 98119
(206) 448-8000
Web site: http://seattlepi.nwsource.com

WEB SITES

Due to the changing nature of Internet links, the Rosen Publishing Group, Inc., has developed an online list of Web sites related to the subject of this book. This site is updated regularly. Please use this link to access the list:

http://www.rosenlinks.com/icb/jebe

FOR FURTHER READING

Brackett, Virginia R. *Jeff Bezos.* New York, NY: Chelsea House, 2001.

Friedman, Mara. *Amazon.com for Dummies.* New York, NY: John Wiley and Sons, Inc., 2004.

Garty, Judy. *Jeff Bezos: Business Genius of Amazon.com.* Berkeley Heights, NJ: Enslow, 2003.

Parks, Peggy J. *Jeff Bezos.* San Diego, CA: Blackbirch, 2005.

Ryan, Bernard. *Jeff Bezos: Business Executive and Founder of Amazon.com.* New York, NY: Facts On File, 2005.

Saunders, Rebecca. *Business the Amazon.com Way.* New York, NY: John Wiley and Sons, Inc., 2002.

Sherman, Josepha. *Jeff Bezos: King of Amazon.com.* Minneapolis, MN: Millbrook, 2001.

Spector, Robert. *Amazon.com: Get Big Fast.* New York, NY: HarperBusiness, 2002.

Acohido, Byron. "Amazon CEO Takes Long View." *USA Today*. July 5, 2005. Retrieved August 2, 2005 (http://www.usatoday.com/money/industries/technology/2005-07-05-amazon-bezos_x.htm).

AskMen.com. "Jeff Bezos: Biography." May 2000. Retrieved April 22, 2005 (http://www.askmen.com/men/may00/26c_jeff_bezos.html).

Bayers, Chip. "The Inner Bezos." *Wired*. July 2003. Retrieved April 9, 2005 (http://wired-vig.wired.com/wired/archive/7.03/bezos_pr.html).

Deutschman, Alan. "Inside the Mind of Jeff Bezos." *Fast Company*. August 2004. Retrieved April 22, 2005 (http://www.fastcompany.com/magazine/85/bezos_2.html).

Fishman, Charles. "Face Time with Jeff Bezos." *Fast Company*, Vol. 43, February 2001, p. 80.

Frey, Christine, and John Cook. "How Amazon.com Survived, Thrived and Turned a Profit." *Seattle Post-Intelligencer*. January 28, 2004. Retrieved July 29, 2005 (http://seattlepi.nwsource.com/business/158315_amazon28.html).

Graczyk, Michael. "West Texas County Abuzz as Bezos Plans Spaceport." *USA Today*. March 14, 2005. Retrieved September 25, 2005 (http://www.usatoday.com/tech/science/space/2005-03-14-bezos-plans-spaceport_x.htm).

Miller, Brian. "Profile: MacKenzie Bezos." *Seattle Weekly*. September 14–20, 2005. Retrieved September 25, 2005 (http://seattleweekly.com/features/0537/050914_fallarts_bezos.php).

Mulady, Kathy. "Recent Layoffs at Area Technology Companies." *Seattle Post-Intelligencer*. January 31, 2001. Retrieved August 14, 2005 (http://seattlepi.nwsource.com/venture/layoff.asp?id=101).

Quittner, Joshua. "1999 Person of the Year: Jeffrey P. Bezos." *Time*. December 27, 1999. Retrieved April 22, 2005 (http://www.time.com/time/boy/bezos4.html).

Sandoval, Greg. "Bezos: Back on Top." CNet News.com. January 23, 2002. Retrieved August 2, 2005 (http://news.com.com/Bezos+Back+on+top/2008-1082_3-821168.html).

Spector, Robert. *Amazon.com: Get Big Fast*. New York, NY: HarperBusiness, 2002.

Wheatley, Malcolm. "Jeff Bezos Takes Everything Personally." *CIO Magazine*. August 1, 2000. Retrieved August 5, 2005 (http://www.cio.com/archives/080100_bezos.html).

Source Notes

Chapter 1

1. Joshua Quittner, "1999 Person of the Year: Jeffrey P. Bezos," *Time*, December 27, 1999. Retrieved April 22, 2005 (http://www.time.com/time/poy/bezos4.html).

2. Quittner.

3. Robert Spector, *Amazon.com: Get Big Fast* (New York: HarperBusiness, 2002), p. 5.

4. Chip Bayers, "The Inner Bezos," *Wired*, July 2003. Retrieved April 9, 2005 (http://wired-vig.wired.com/wired/archive/7.03/bezos_pr.html).

5. Bayers.

Chapter 2

1. Robert Spector, *Amazon.com: Get Big Fast* (New York: HarperBusiness, 2002), p. 12.

2. Joshua Quittner, "1999 Person of the Year: Jeffrey P. Bezos," *Time*, December 27, 1999. Retrieved April 22, 2005 (http://www.time.com/time/poy/bezos4.html).

3. "Jeff Bezos: Biography," AskMen.com, May 2000. Retrieved April 22, 2005 (http://www.askmen.com/men/may00/26c_jeff_bezos.html).

4. Charles Fishman, "Face Time with Jeff Bezos," *Fast Company*, Vol. 43, February 2001, p. 80; Spector, p. 87.

5. Quittner.

6. Quittner.

CHAPTER 3

1. Robert Spector, *Amazon.com: Get Big Fast* (New York: HarperBusiness, 2002), p. 33.

2. The Nile River is longer than the Amazon, but the Amazon and its tributaries carry more water than the Nile and its tributaries.

3. Spector, p. 53.

4. Joshua Quittner, "1999 Person of the Year: Jeffrey P. Bezos," *Time*, December 27, 1999. Retrieved April 22, 2005 (http://www.time. com/time/poy/bezos4.html).

5. Quittner.

6. Spector, pp. 73–74, 84.

7. Christine Frey and John Cook, "How Amazon.com Survived, Thrived and Turned a Profit," *Seattle Post-Intelligencer*, January 28, 2004. Retrieved July 29, 2005 (http://seattlepi. nwsource.com/business/158315_ amazon28.html).

CHAPTER 4

1. Robert Spector, *Amazon.com: Get Big Fast* (New York: HarperBusiness, 2002), p. 138.

2. Alan Deutschman, "Inside the Mind of Jeff Bezos," *Fast Company*, August 2004. Retrieved

April 22, 2005. (http://www.fastcompany.com/
magazine/85/bezos_2.html).

CHAPTER 5

1. Byron Acohido, "Amazon CEO Takes Long
   View," *USA Today*, July 5, 2005. Retrieved
   August 2, 2005. (http://www.usatoday.com/
   money/industries/technology/2005-07-05-
   amazon-bezos_x.htm).

2. Greg Sandoval, "Bezos: Back on Top," CNet
   News.com, January 23, 2002. Retrieved August
   2, 2005 (http://news.com.com/Bezos+Back+on+
   top/2008-1082_3-821168.html).

3. Acohido.

4. Kathy Mulady, "Recent Layoffs at Area
   Technology Companies," *Seattle Post-
   Intelligencer*, January 31, 2001. Retrieved
   August 14, 2005 (http://seattlepi.nwsource.com/
   venture/ layoff.asp?id=101).

5. Acohido.

6. Chip Bayers, "The Inner Bezos," *Wired*, July
   2003. Retrieved April 9, 2005 (http://wired-vig.
   wired.com/wired/archive/7.03/bezos_pr.html).

INDEX

ABOUT THE AUTHOR

Ann Byers lives in California, where she writes and edits young adult books. She also works with the Entrepreneurial Training Program of the Central Valley Business Incubator, where she helps aspiring entrepreneurs start their own businesses. She has watched many people develop visions, design plans, and work to make companies profitable. Ann hopes that some day, one of her students will be the next Jeff Bezos.

PHOTO CREDITS

Designer: Nelson Sa
Editor: Christopher Roberts
Photo Researcher: Gabriel Caplan